100 PLUS TRICKS FOR QUICK LEARNING ALL YOUR STUDENTS' NAMES

DR DHEERAJ MEHROTRA

Copyright © Dr Dheeraj Mehrotra
All Rights Reserved.

Contents

Preface

"100 Plus Tricks for Quick Learning All your students' names" is a work of great interest and a priority for all educators globally. In the present educational scenario, the role of the teacher is more of a facilitator than the role that the teacher played earlier when the teacher was the only spokesperson whose instructions the students had to follow verbatim, being passive listeners. The teacher now leads the children toward self-learning; they identify their learning styles, interests, backgrounds and abilities and work accordingly.

We must explore this to build rapport among our students as educators.

Happy Learning & Cheers!

www.authordheerajmehrotra.com

ONE

100 Plus Tricks

One of the surveys suggested the following Tricks to remember the students' names as the best way forward to engage them and explore the teaching and learning of these kids with joy and fellowship. It is essential to learn and use your students' names since it helps create a more relaxed and casual environment in the classroom and demonstrates an interest in your pupils as unique persons.

Educators who make an effort to memorise their students' names in big beginning classes might help alleviate the feelings of anonymity and isolation that are common among the student body. The use of student names has been shown to build classroom community, increase student engagement by helping them feel more comfortable, make students feel more accountable to the instructor, ensure students are comfortable seeking help, and increase student satisfaction with a course (Cooper et. al 2017, Murdoch et.

Instead of using the roll number for collecting attendance, each person's name is spoken aloud.

❧❧❧

For the first few classes, have students write their names in huge characters on both sides of a folded 5 x 8 index card and put it on their desks.

❧❧❧

Each pupil needs to hear their name shouted aloud. They will have a sense of self-assurance, encouraging them to approach the teachers and discuss any issues or successes they have had.

ᏅᏅᏅ

When you initially greet the class, take a few additional seconds to ask each kid to mention his or her most 12 notable physical attributes or other distinguishing characteristics.

ᏅᏅᏅ

Include methods to pronounce names that are foreign to you.

❦❦❦

Connect with them over social media and like their posts.

❦❦❦

Call them by their first name every time you meet them by asking their names.

ᐅᐅᐅ

Let them wear their first name for a few days as a TAG on their shirts/uniforms.

ᐅᐅᐅ

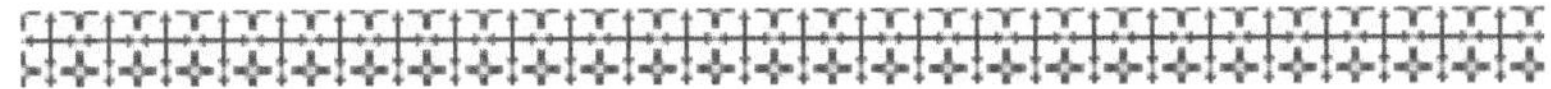

Make them wear the HAT or a CAP with their first name.

ᐅᐅᐅ

Let them wear the T-Shirt with their first name at the front or the back.

ᐻᐻᐻ

Ask them to write their name on the board at least once weekly.

ᐻᐻᐻ

Ask them to bring and make a collage of their family pictures and put them in the class as OUR FAMILY.

ᗡᗡᗡ

You are responsible for taking attendance daily in charge of a classroom. It is simple to keep in mind. For the other classes, it takes a little bit more time. Every pupil possesses a one-of-a-kind personality and a range of facial expressions. I pay attention to them in a way that allows me to learn their names.

ᗡᗡᗡ

Because I work with college students, I asked them to give me an unfiltered selfie with their names written on it. This will allow me to begin associating names with faces. They were rewarded with additional points, and there was no obligation on their part.

ᐯᐯᐯ

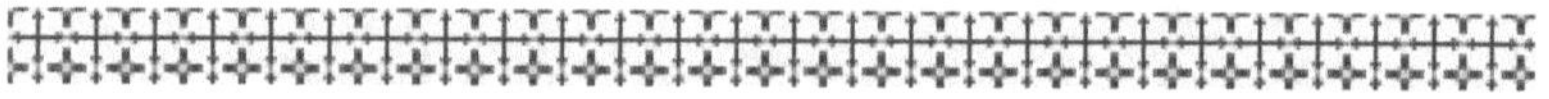

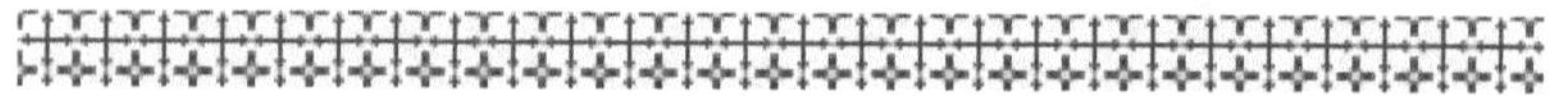

Because I have excellent recall... it shouldn't be too difficult to memorise people's names.

❧❧❧

Keeping them in the order of the alphabet and calling out their name several times, and then whoopee!

ԾԾԾ

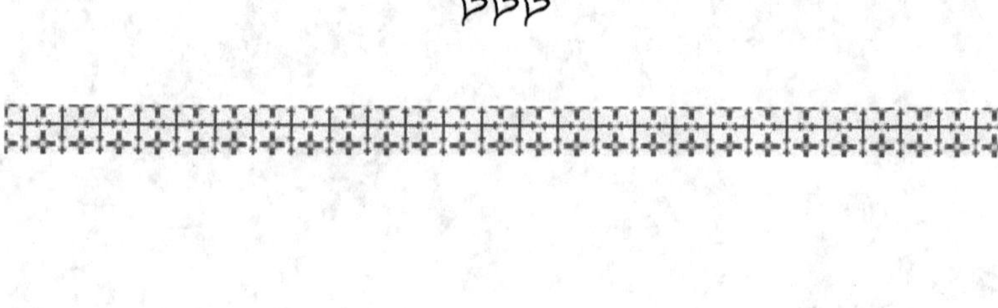

Play Name Games with kids.

ԾԾԾ

Have students arrange themselves alphabetically and ask them to say a poem.

ԾԾԾ

Use their names whenever possible.

ÞÞÞ

Ask them to tell their stories using their name as one of the characters.

ÞÞÞ

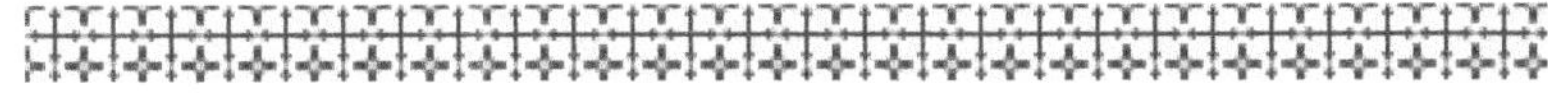

Associate the name with similar words or words that rhyme.

ᐅᐅᐅ

Use mnemonics and associations to remember the name.

ᐅᐅᐅ

Engage with the name via some activity.

ᐅᐅᐅ

Pay attention when some child introduces.

ᏢᏢᏢ

Repeating each person's name daily during the teaching and learning process. You will slowly recover your memory. They also have a sense of significance.

ᏢᏢᏢ

Unconditional love should be shown to youngsters. The names will be registered on your behalf automatically. It might take anything from four to ten days, but so can falling in love with someone for real.

ᏢᏢᏢ

Ask pupils to sit in the same spot for a few courses to help them remember their names faster.

ϸϸϸ

During the first class, take images of their pupils individually or in small groups and ask them to put their names on the shots. Alternatively, request that students bring a photocopy of their student ID photo to be attached to a seating chart or roster.

ᎮᎮᎮ

Assign seats with their names prominently displayed, identify each area with their name, and make an effort to become acquainted with them. It was usually more accessible for me to remember other things associated with their names when I participated in those first-day and back-to-school activities to get to know what they love doing, etc. The very best of luck to you!!

ᎮᎮᎮ

An essential thing in the world is unrestricted love, take care of their belongings, make their places with their images and the first name.

ᗞᗞᗞ

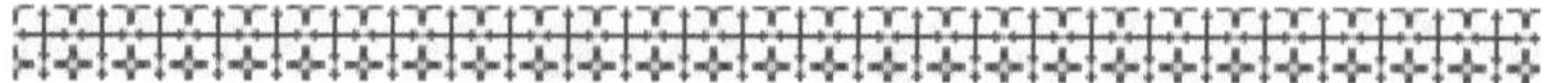

After the first person has introduced themselves, I will state their name again.
When the second person introduces myself, I repeat the first name and then submit the second person, and so on...
After they have all completed their work, I will repeat all of the words.
Afterwards, they were required to switch positions about where they were seated.
While they are completing the mixing portion of the process, I keep repeating their statements at least three to four times.
If I execute it successfully, they are obligated to praise me.
And they are obligated to award me a perfect score!

ᗞᗞᗞ

The end, as they say.

Keeping a close eye on the daily attendance list. Learn 5-10 names every session before and after class.

Invite kids to your office in small groups to discover more about them than just their names.

Both techniques demonstrate that you are concerned about the needs of individual

pupils.

ᛈᛈᛈ

In my opinion, there is no catch. When I was a pupil, I always pondered how my instructors could remember each of our names. Now that I think about it, the fact that we spend most of our time with them could be the reason.

ᛈᛈᛈ

Ask students to give you anything about themselves or their names that will help you remember them, such as where they are from, what they enjoy reading or do for pleasure or their long-term aspirations.

ᛈᛈᛈ

Using their names as an example to answer inquiries about the issue. It performs pretty nicely.

ᐯᐯᐯ

After spending a few days with my children for the first time, it was only natural for me to eventually recall their names. You do not require the use of many techniques. When I started working in this field in 2011, the students' comments they learned from me were still ingrained in my memory.

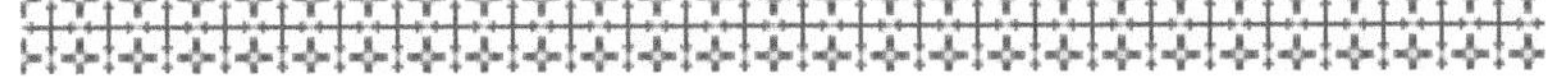

I put the parents' phone numbers in a file next to each student's name.

Allow kids 2-3 minutes in pairs to interview each other and uncover something

"no one will ever forget."

Allow around 1 minute for each couple as you go around the room, asking students to identify themselves.

ᐅᐅᐅ

Source: Times of India, NIE Edition

When they took their roll no. Wise
In the process of collecting attendance, I will be
calling out the name.
The act of providing them with copies of their works...
Using their names when discussing Grammar is a
great way to show respect.

We could put their names on name tags, laminate
them, and request that they wear them every day...

You might try pronouncing their words in the order of the alphabet.

I use this activity as an icebreaker in the classroom by asking the students to introduce themselves using an adjective that begins with the first letter of their name. For example, Abhinav may describe Aishwarya as being affectionate. When they were finished, I asked one of them to list all words corresponding to the adjectives they had mentioned.

As a result, pupils acquire new adverbs, and I, too, get familiar with their names.

1) When taking attendance, call pupils by their names rather than their roll numbers.

2) Make a connection between the face and the name. It has been demonstrated to be an effective method for encoding information into memories.

3) Instead of referring to pupils in the classroom as the guy on the third bench or the girl on the final bench when asking for replies during class hours, try to address individuals by their full names whenever possible.

If you cannot recall their names, you should inquire about them until you can do so.

These tried-and-true approaches will help you remember the names of kids in five or six different classes, not just for the remainder of this school year but for the rest of your life. To everyone in our teaching community, best wishes and more power to you!

Good day to everybody!

On the first day, I decided to learn everyone's names by playing a game called "name chain."

Please hand in all of the notebooks, and then call the kids' names to have them returned to them when you've checked their names.

Share your name with them.

ϸϸϸ

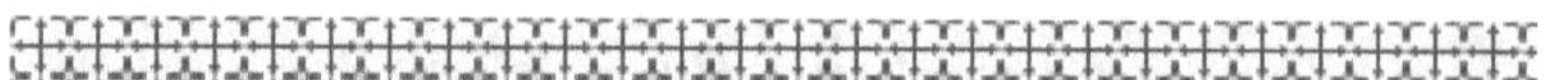

A person's name is associated with a physical characteristic.

With visual representations, you may often tie the name (or key phrases with similar sounds) to something more meaningful and authentic.

For example, imagine a tall, slender student called Sumit carrying a heavy crate of flowers on his head.

Some Requisites on Motivating Kids within classrooms and for Home Study:

Choosing the Correct Environment and explore play as an essential par of the child's learning and towards enhancing the early development of the kids.

ᗶᗶᗶ

Finding a quiet and private space to study in order to avoid distractions is the first step in improving attention. We need to ensure our curriculum content matches school areas of focus with creativity, critical thinking, communication, confidence and collaboration.

ᗶᗶᗶ

Be well-organized. Kids need to be told:

Before they begin studying, make certain that they have all of their study materials and that the area in which they sit is clean and healthy.

ᗶᗶᗶ

Distractions should be avoided.

ÞÞÞ

To boost their seating capacity, unplug any unwanted equipment when studying.

ÞÞÞ

Maintain the routine

If they decide to set a schedule, stick to it. Change their routines on a regular basis since this might cause confusion.

ÞÞÞ

Breaks

Take enough pauses while studying to refresh your thoughts and rejuvenate your body. Take at least 10-15 minutes of a break every 3 hours.

ÞÞÞ

Proper nutrition and rest are essential.

These two are crucial. A good diet promotes physical fitness, mental wellness, and illness prevention. It is recommended to avoid eating junk food during tests and to consume more fruits and beverages in between study sessions. While 7-8 hours of sleep is recommended to keep the mind sharp and eliminate drowsiness.

ᐅᐅᐅ

TWO
PARENTING TIPS

First, have faith in your parental abilities. Relish the privilege of being a parent. Hold your head up and keep in shape. Headaches are caused by good parenting, whereas heartaches result from poor parenting.

Second, get ready for the most difficult task: To be a parent is the most challenging work you have ever done or will ever undertake. Prepare to have your mind blown by the trade secrets you're about to discover. Always aim to be ready for everything.

Learn the "how to" of baby care; this is Secret #3.

The responsibility of parenting starts with pregnancy. You can't continue smoking or drinking after you find out you're expecting. Both tea and coffee should be avoided. You know the drill: Eat right, get enough sleep, etc. There is a wealth of knowledge to be gained from the experiences of other parents, especially if you are a first-time parent. There is a wealth of knowledge that your parents may impart.

Avoid becoming a chronic complainer; this is Secret No. 5.

Even if your kid isn't listening, that's no reason to start whining. A child's pride is damaged when you criticise them. Good parents love their children for who they are now, not for what they could become.

Tip #6: Always have high expectations for your child. This is a particular method to instil pride and accomplishment in your offspring. To be a good parent, one must let one's children take on the consequences of their actions.

Key No. 7: Prompt your kid to take some calculated dangers Because taking chances is essential to one's growth, you should encourage your child to do so within limits. Our children should be respected as full members of society, not lesser adults.

Do not instantly respond when your youngster commits a mistake; this is Secret #8. Be sure to do some serious thinking before you act. No matter what, you should always love your child. We've all erred and will continue to do so; nobody's flawless.

Tip #9: Help your kids feel strong by showing them how. Don't make life simpler for your child; instead, instil in him the value of struggle as a guiding principle.

Tenth Tip: Don't sugarcoat anything; instead, teach your kid the truth about the world. The following behaviours may indicate that your child is putting you to the test: a temper tantrum, rage, sobbing, or disrespect. Leave the room and tell him you'll have to discuss this with him later.

Rule # 11: Don't ignore your child when he or she wants to talk. Put down your gadgets and give him your full attention. You should wait until he finishes talking before voicing your view. Rather than being soft and mushy, be challenging and respectful. Don't wait for your kid to initiate a conversation; instead, have one with him or her. Prompt him with questions and wait for an answer. I become envious when you constantly compare me to other kids, so please stop doing that.

Tip #13: Never cut off a call from your child; always make time for conversation—the parent-child relationship benefits from both parties being able to communicate their needs and receive them.

Tip #14 Use Your Head: Do your best to instil a sense of good and wrong in your students. Get them to stop doing destructive and more of the right. Never use the threat of abandonment as a motivational tool with your child.

Truth #15 Always Abide by Your Regulations Whenever you establish a regulation, you should always uphold it. How can you expect your child to behave correctly if you don't? Ignore any begging, crying, demanding, and pouting.

Trick #16: Be a good example for your child. You should never engage in inappropriate behaviour in front of youngsters. Do not let your child see you lose control of your emotions by expressing anger, annoyance, etc., in front of them (believe me, children are good at imitating).

Truth #18 Allow imitation: Imitation is the primary means by which humans learn. Facilitate imitation-based learning of new skills.

Unspeakable Truth #19: Children aren't great at understanding the nuances of language. That's why empty words like "I love you" do not affect them. Whether via words, actions, or presents, let them know how much they mean to you.

Twenty-Third-Secret-Be-Positive If you are optimistic, your child will be, too. The fact that you failed at something doesn't mean you should dwell on it. Instead of shouting at me, Mom and Dad fixed my mistakes. You mustn't be a negative role model to prevent your child from becoming a pessimistic adult like you. Your child won't pick up your bad attitude if you model positivity for them.

To comprehend that you are a safe place for your child is the 22nd and last secret. They should feel secure in your company. Foster a sense of security in your youngster. If you want your youngster to depend on you,

Secret #23 is to earn his or her trust. If he tells you something, you shouldn't tell anyone, not your partner. The lessons you learned as a child can serve you well as a parent. Take what you like and go with it. It makes sense to steer clear of whatever it was that gave you a negative experience.

No. 25: Teach your child from your own experiences. Don't hold back from sharing your life lessons with your offspring; explain how you dealt with challenges, acted in social situations, and fed yourself through the years.

ppp

About The Author

Dheeraj Mehrotra, MS, MPhil, PhD (Education Management) honoris causa., a white and a yellow belt in SIX SIGMA, a Certified NLP Business Diploma holder, is an Educational Innovator, Author, with expertise in Six Sigma In Education, Academic Audits, Neuro-Linguistic Programming (NLP), Total Quality Management In Education, an Experiential Educator, *a CBSE Resource towards School Assessment (SQAA), CCE, JIT, Five S, and KAIZEN.*

He has authored over 100 books on topics which include Computer Science, AI, Digital Body Language, NLP, Quality Circles, School Management, Classroom Effectiveness and Safety and security in schools. A former Principal at De Indian Public School, New Delhi, (INDIA), NPS International School, Guwahati, and Education Officer at GEMS, Gurgaon, with an ample teaching experience of over Two Decades, he is a certified Trainer for Quality Circles/ TQM in Education and QCI Standards for School Accreditation/ School Audits and Management. He has also been honoured with the President of India's National Teacher Award in the year 2006 and the Best Science Teacher State Award (By the Ministry of Science and Technology, State of UP), Innovation in Education for his inception of Six Sigma In Education by Education Watch, New Delhi and Education World-Best Teacher Award, BOLT Learner Teacher Award by Air India, 'Innovation in Education Award 2016' by Higher Education Forum (HEF), Gujarat Chapter, among others. He has developed over 150 FREE EDUCATIONAL MOBILE Apps for the Google Play Store exclusively for Teachers, Students, and Parents.

This work has been recognised by the LIMCA BOOK OF RECORDS & INDIA BOOK OF RECORDS as the only Indian to draw that feast. Dr Mehrotra works as a PRINCIPAL at KUNWARS GLOBAL SCHOOL, Lucknow, in India. He has conducted over 1000 workshops globally on "Excellence In Education" integrated with Total Quality Management and Six Sigma, Technology Integration in Education (TIE), Developing towards being ROCKSTAR TEACHERS, including Cyberspace, Cyber Security, Classroom Management, School Leadership & Management, and Innovative teaching within classrooms via Mind Maps, NLP and Experiential Learning in Academics. He is an active TEDx speaker and can be viewed on the youtube TEDx channel.

As a premium UDEMY Instructor, he has developed over 450 courses and caters to over 8 Lakh students from 180 countries.

He can be visited at www.authordheerajmehrotra.com.

Books By The Same Author

Social
Skills for
Educators
Dr Dheeraj Mehrotra

Now on
#AMAZON
FINANCIAL
LITERACY
IN SCHOOLS
DR DHEERAJ
MEHROTRA